I0408523

How to Cure Depression.

How to Overcome Depression and Anxiety, How to Understand Depression, A Training Guide and Solutions to Combat Depression, Getting Rid of Stress and Low Self-Esteem.

By:

Tomas Hensley

Copyright © 2017 by [Tomas Hensley]. All Rights Reserved.

All rights reserved. No part of this guide may be reproduced in any form without permission in writing from the publisher except in the case of brief quotations embodied in critical articles or reviews.

Legal & Disclaimer

The information contained in this book and its contents is not designed to replace or take the place of any form of medical or professional advice; and is not meant to replace the need for independent medical, financial, legal or other professional advice or services, as may be required.

Table of Contents

Introduction

Do you know someone who is depressed and cannot seem to get over it? Do you often feel a sense of tiredness, powerlessness and lack of interest in your life? Chances are, you may be depressed, but there's good news.

Millions of people have beaten depression. They have come back as stronger personalities than before – *and so can you!*

Depression happens as a response or reaction when someone suffers discouragement, defeat or disappointment.

But, depression is more than just sadness or a bad mood.

When someone is sad for more than a couple of weeks to the extent that the feeling interferes with the regular activities of living, then the person is said to be depressed, and this condition requires medical attention.

Anyone who is depressed really needs help getting over it, because it affects work, family, life and studies. Many people who are depressed do not seek professional help. This is indeed bad.

This Book is your comprehensive guide to understanding depression, diagnosing yourself and then walking the path towards a sustainable cure in an effective and guaranteed way.

Welcome to a life-changing read that will bring you back to a normal, happy life. Seek help and the rest is destined for good.

Chapter I: The Basics

Depression is more than just a sad mood. It is an unexplainable glum feeling that never goes away. Every kind of depression is connected in one way or the other to the absence of a specific need fulfillment.

Depression occurs when a person loses the sense of belonging, self-control, self-esteem, and a sense of meaningful existence.

When a person is depressed, the part of the brain that deals with pain management is activated. The pain management system activated by the brain is meant to help the depressed person cope with the underlying situation. **Coping mechanisms differ between people.** In short, there is a total change in the brain chemistry of the depressed. Several coping mechanisms and mannerisms tend to be hard to accept for those who are living with the depressed. Life gets tricky for the depressed and for those who live with the depressed.

Types of depression

Feeling down once in a while is not really depression. However, when the condition continues it definitely is classifiable as clinical depression. These are different types of depression:

1. Situational depression
2. Atypical depression
3. Premenstrual Dysphoric Disorder (PMDD)
4. Peripartum depression
5. Postpartum depression
6. Psychotic depression
7. Seasonal affective disorder (SAD)
8. Bipolar disorder
9. Persistent depressive disorder
10. Major Depression

While a low mood is common for each of the above mentioned depression types, the duration of depression and the associated signs and symptoms varies for each of these depression types.

Causes of depression

Depression is mainly caused by changes in life circumstances, grief, stress, alterations in hormone levels, medical conditions, and several other traumatic and overwhelming demands of life. These factors alter the brain chemistry. The onset of depression and its expression differs among people. How people deal with depression is in part influenced by their genetic patterns.

Signs and Symptoms

The coping mechanism of the depressed is expressed by feelings of anger, helplessness, unworthiness, sadness, and alienation. They tend to be more aggressive to people around them. They internally feel abandoned and rejected. They remove themselves from people and things. They have a hard time to let go. They lose interest in things that were once their favorite.

In some cases, depression can combine with bipolar disorder and a range of other psychiatric issues. Extreme untreated cases can even lead to conditions like schizophrenia. However, a majority of the depression cases are anywhere from mild to moderate, which is treatable with appropriate counseling and life style changes.

Can depression cause future life complications?

Everyone, regardless of age, gender, occupation, wealth, status and social disposition, tend to become depressed at some point in time. Some take to the healing quickly. However, if left untreated, depression can cause short-term and long-term life complications that hinder routine activity and performance of the affected person, apart from causing other debilitating diseases.

Short-term side effects of depression are unexplained pain, aches in different parts of the body, loss of weight, increase in weight, changes in sleep patterns, problems with libido, and decreased sexual activity. For some people, it becomes a long-term life complication.

It is common for non-depressed people to experience one or more of these symptoms. However, when clusters of such symptoms tend to continue for over more than a couple of weeks, this is a sure sign of depression that needs to be treated.

Short-term depression when untreated or dealt with, can become a "here to stay thing" and the patient can develop "long-term life complications". This can lead to a negative impact in the functional aspects of life. The person who is depressed for the long-term will have trouble concentrating, trouble making decisions, and difficulty remembering things.

In cases of severe depression, they can develop delusions and hallucinations. When not cared for, they can become involved in substance abuse, miss work commitments, miss school commitments, and they even keep away from other people. Suicide and violent behavior is also seen in cases involving chronic stress. Some patterns of aggressive behavior are expressed as verbal harm or physical harm to other people.

Chapter II: Diagnose Yourself

It is possible for you to diagnose yourself for depression right now. So, let's do it!

If you are feeling moody and hopeless for majority of your productive and leisure hours, then you need to verify if one or more of the conditions **given below** prove true in your case. If you say one or more of the following are true **for more than a period of two weeks**, you can call yourself depressed to a certain degree:

- Feeling low, irritable, moody and hopeless for nearly everyday
- Not interested in executing activities of daily living for more than a period of two weeks
- Not interested in socializing
- Not interested in continuing with regular leisure activities
- Unable to fall asleep
- Feeling sleepy all day
- Feeling restless
- Loss of appetite
- Weight loss
- Weight gain due to binge eating
- Low energy level
- Feeling bad about yourself
- Feel you are a failure
- Letting your family members down
- Unable to concentrate on school work
- Unable to concentrate on activities like reading and watching TV
- Your activities slow down too much to the extent of people noticing the slow down
- Tend to be too fidgety and restless
- Feeling like you would be better off dead
- Hurting and putting yourself down in one way or the other
- Feeling suicidal

Even if you feel like no one is there to help you, it is high time you reach out for help. Help is always there when you genuinely seek it out. *The intensity of depression and the degree of help you might need is something that your physician might be able to help you with.* It should be noted that there are different types of depressive symptoms. Some are mild. Some are very serious and need hardcore help and close monitoring.

Talking to the person who is suspected of being depressed is the most common diagnostic tool used by the doctors. Those who are trained to help with depression are the best people to give you the solution you are looking for.

What now?

If you have self-diagnosed yourself with depression using the self-assessment list you might want to check if you have been living in environmental conditions that nurture depression by reading below.

Long-term depression can lead to borderline personality disorder (BPD). Borderline personality disorder is a condition that is caused due to long term depression triggers that the person is unable to control. This is a mental condition that can be serious and it is mostly characterized by unstable mood, unstable behavior, and unstable relationships. There is a considerable amount of genetic component to BPD.

BPD is very commonly seen in people who grow up in a neglectful environment. These people have been exposed to lots of abusive and unstable situations in life without anyone to guide them to stable decision making. They have had to deal with many situations that were above and beyond what can be normally done by people of their age. This eventually leads to BPD.

Those who have a borderline personality disorder tend to show patterns of bizarre and unstable moods. They are impulsive with a poor self-image about themselves. They have bizarre behavior patterns. These behavior patterns happen in situations where the person has been chronically subject to demeaning experiences. They were expected to handle more than what they were capable of handling. They were forced to shoulder a heavier burden than they could handle.

Serotonin is an important hormone that regulates mood. There is a visible fluctuation in serotonin levels in these patients, which makes them more susceptible to BPD.

They tend to idealize a relationship or they devalue a relationship. This in part is due to the long list of unhappy experiences dealing with people who expected more and more from them. They have crossed extreme situations as children. Most people with BPD have been children who were verbally and emotionally abused. They tend to have been pretty vulnerable as children. They had to play adults while they were children. They were misguided.

They are scared of imaginary abandonment or actual abandonment. They try to avoid abandonment of any kind. They have difficulty controlling anger. Due to an unstable self-image, they tend to spend too much money. They become vulnerable to taking drugs and other substances of abuse.

They experience frequent mood swings. They have trouble controlling their anger. They are angry all the time. They exhibit anger at all times. They land up getting in to physical abuse and physical fights very often.

In extreme cases of stress, they even develop paranoia. They experience severe disassociation.

People who are identified as positive for BPD need to get help. They might require psychotherapy or even hospitalization. The physician will study the emotional and behavioral history of the patient and offer treatment accordingly.

The physician will identify unhealthy beliefs, behaviors and inappropriate perceptions present in the person and they will choose to offer behavioral therapy as needed by offering:

- Cognitive therapy
- Dialectal therapy
- Schema focused therapy customized for the patient

In many cases of BPD, the person is not aware of the unreasonable belief and behavioral patterns they exhibit. They believe it is normal to be the way they are. They probably never had an opportunity, mental disposition, or training to understand the acceptable pattern of behavior. When they are helped to recognize these behavioral patterns, they accept it and they learn to respond in a healthy way.

They learn to view the world in a positive way. They learn to get away from negative situations. They learn how to embrace life with a positive life style. They learn to maintain cool.

When to Consult a Doctor?

There is no early time to consult with a doctor for depression; the earlier the better. You need not become gloomy with depression to ask for a consultation. The more you procrastinate, the more you are losing the benefits of a consultation. If you have the slightest doubt that you are depressed, it is good to nip it in the bud.

Chapter III: A word on prevention

Writing down your anger and regret is one way to prevent depression in routine life.

Depression is a manifestation of one's inability to achieve or gain something. It is the inability of the brain to cope with a specific failure pattern when one had high expectations of winning. The brain simply cannot wait to react to something that might be unacceptable. However, due to social reasons, you might not express yourselves well in certain situations.

Several minor and major coping mechanisms in life triggered by high stress situations use a coping strategy of withholding feelings. These then accumulate over time.

Feelings of aggression when suppressed tend to remain dormant in your memory. Then when the environmental factors affect it enough, the result is aggressive behavior, crying episodes, and yelling to tear the roof off.

Aggression is actually a major expression of unexpressed depressive episodes and hard feelings locked inside the brain, routinely over years.

A simple way of dealing with routine depression is to write out your regrets on a piece of paper without editing your feelings, without any kind of fear of judgment, criticism, and condemnation from others.

Once you are done writing it, read it through and tear it up. It is only for you to get over the hard feelings. This writing is not an evaluation of moral ethics. You can swear in the writing if you want to.

The recipient can be your parent, employer, spouse, children, neighbor, a system or anything. Cry out loud in the paper by simply writing down your feelings. You will be relieved. You will get an idea of what is eating you from inside. You will develop positive patterns for dealing with tough situations that would otherwise lead to depression. This is a method of clearing the recycle bin in your head.

Essential lifestyle tips

The opposite of depression is happiness. It is important that you stay relaxed and happy all the time. Sometimes even pretending that you are happy can eventually make staying happy a habit.

Worrying and yapping about stuff tends to make it a second behavior and it does happen that even during happy times, you have trouble being relaxed and happy.

When it is time to be happy be happy. When it is time to worry be worried. When it is time to recover, do recover from grief.

It is all about what you train your mind to do. Learn to switch over your brain to suit the actual reality and demands of life.

We all know what makes a good life style. It starts with good health. Have a healthy diet, have a healthy financial structure, insure yourself, save for your retirement, work enough, go out on a vacation, and have friends. Most important of all you do not want to abuse tobacco, alcohol or drugs. You do not want to practice anything that will definitely harm your well-being in the long run.

"8 hours of work, 8 hours of rest, 8 hours of recreation."

We re-create our lives every day. You need 8 hours a day to make preparations for the next day, to cook and plan your meals, to exercise, to watch TV, to enjoy being with friends and to socialize. If you thought that life is about working 24 hours a day, you will surely crash one day. Healthy work life balance is crucial to be able to stay relaxed and happy. Practice contentment.

Be realistic in your expectations. Plan life and take life as it comes. Surprises and shocks are unavoidable. Just accept that you will have to face unknown events. You will be able to get over it. Have a routine and things will fall in to place.

How to prevent depression after a big life event?

The death of a loved one is the biggest depressive episode one has to go through. The situation is too mind-eating to deal with. This can be related to loss of a spouse, loss of child, loss of parents, loss of a closest friend, loss of a pet, or loss of anyone whom one has considered close to your heart.

"Grieving is the first and essential step to preventing major depression...

A minor phase of depression in reality is unavoidable..."

We do not want depression to progress to chronic depression or major depression, thereby ruining the overall quality of the individual after the loss of a loved one.

It is okay to grieve. However, it is not okay to get too depressed. Though grieving and being depressed appear to be kind of the same, they are different. It should be noted that people grieve in different ways. Not all grieving or depressive episodes are similar.

All of a sudden, everyone around you is giving you heaps of tips and tricks to gain strength to deal with the loss. In reality, the loss of any loved one is not an easy situation to deal with. Unless you are extremely strong and trained to be strong in the worse situations in life, a period of grief is unavoidable. Depressive episodes are unavoidable too.

Getting lot of sleep is the first step. The brain has undergone a traumatic episode dealing with the shock related to the loss of a loved one. The brain networks tend to go haywire because someone who was there to command the activities and to do the agenda for the day is gone forever. The brain needs lot of sleep to rewire and reprogram itself. It needs to heal itself to deal with the massive change ahead. The brain needs to know about how to come up with a new to-do life pattern.

Grieving is grieving and you have to grieve. You cannot pretend that nothing has happened. You cannot behave normally when things are not really normal.

When you lose a loved one, you are losing a major platform in life. Even if the rest of the world is there around you to shoulder you for the rest of your life, something within you will be unable to accept the reality. You will need support during this time, even if you feel you don't need any help.

You will develop feelings of guilt, feelings of being a burden to others, feelings of hopelessness and a lot more. The only thing you can do now is to accept what has happened and to simply experience the feelings that are happening to you.

The range of coping mechanisms you might go through might be talking about your loved one over and over again, crying over memories, visiting with people who mean the most to your loved one, and lots of other stuff. You might not even want to give away your loved ones belongings. It is okay about whatever you are feeling. Just experience the feelings.

You might have to go through a period of denial, where you are still unable to accept the loss. You might be hoping to see your loved one calling you over to your mobile, you might be hoping to see your loved one opening the doors of your house, and you might be imagining they have left for the office or school and a range of other feelings of denial and unbelief. This is experienced by everyone who has undergone a tragic loss.

You will feel numb. You might feel too sad. You might land up feeling guilty about eating without having to cook for your loved one. You might be too tired or guilty to take care of yourself. You might even want to deny the activities of daily living.

The intensity of the shock is very strong. You might not be able to accept any change to your environment. You will want to somehow get back to the normal days being with your loved one. The hard core truth is that things are never going to be same again. The experiences and feelings of denial, numbness, and shock are essential grieving experiences that you should go through without any kind of judgment and embarrassment about yourself. These experiences are important to help you deal with the intensity of the loss.

However, you do not want to allow the grieving process to take over and interfere with your overall personality type and productivity. You do not want the grief pattern and intensity of shock to take over your brain in a way that grief doesn't go away at all. Experiencing acute periods of grief for a short time is acceptable. However, if it is not going away, you need help.

Complicated grief normally takes over when you are not experiencing the feelings of grief. It is important for you to allow yourself to feel sad. You have to force and allow yourself to sleep and eat healthy regardless of how unworthy you feel about yourself. Regardless of whether you or happy or sad, it is important to have a healthy diet. A healthy diet is a fundamental human necessity, regardless of circumstances. It is a great way to help you get over the grief process and stop it from escalating to a complicated depressive phase. If you feel you can, take some counseling. However, you should not be forced to take counseling. In many cases, you might not be able to take in the facts given to you during the counseling. However, your brain is listening and it knows how to integrate the help into your life.

You need not feel bad about crying about it to your friends, family, or counselors. You might feel sorry to cry and worry about the loss to your near ones. It is okay to be that way for some time. With some trained help, you will learn how to get over it.

And you need to remember that everything is normal everywhere. Depression is in your head. All you need to be doing is to set your mind to live your life without your loved one. After all we are not living an everlasting life. We are set to go to the other world on the day the lord has pre-destined for us to die. We are just living and traveling to that day by passing through several experiences. You do not want to paint your journey to death filled with a decade long depression. You want to leave the world with memories. Create memories and create a great life. The world is made up of millions of people.

Millions and millions are born and all the millions who are born will die one day! We are also going to be gone one day. Do not fail yourself by grieving yourself into a major depression. Live your life. Try to come out and accept help, you will heal.

Chapter IV: Management Options

Have you ever been in a situation where you react to a specific situation in a way you never wanted to? Many times, these feelings and words burst out as a result of long-term suppression of your feelings.

You might not feel comfortable about the fact that you had to express certain feelings in a certain way. These feelings might be those you chose to keep within yourselves for social reasons. After you have reacted, you feel sad and depressed about your reactions. This can make you temporarily depressed. It can even make you wonder if you have are bipolar.

Over-the-counter drugs are those drugs that a customer can buy from the pharmacy without any prescription. Over-the-counter depression medications can be sought when you are going through triggers of transient depression.

Reactive depression is a common response to the outburst of a harsh argument.

A single dosage of an OTC drug will help dealing with the follow up stressors of such situations. Amitriptyline, Elavil, Citalopram, Celexa, Lexapro, Doxepin Adapine, Sinquan, Fluoxetine, Prozac, Nortriptyline, Aventyl, Paroxetine, Paxil, Trazodone, Desyrel, or Trialodine are common OTC anti-depressants you can take to help with transient depression.

Reactive depression is very common in women who are going through Premenstrual Dysphoric Disorder (PMSD). If you are a woman reading this, you already know what it feels like.

Have you ever experienced a feeling of general discontent and anxiety? Have you gone through sudden crying spells? Have you ever felt inside like you wanted to cry, although you are not sure why you are crying and you're over-reacting to a specific situation? These are very common symptoms of transient depressive episodes.

Depressive episodes happen when any kind of illness, life-event or accident presses the person to shoulder more than manageable responsibilities.

No matter what the depressive issues are, it is possible to achieve calm. No matter how bad things are, there is hope, and there is healing.

Depressive episodes can occur in combination with pain in different areas of the body like the breasts, muscles, abdomen, back, joints, and pelvis.

There are many people who know they are going through a phase of depression. They prefer not to take prescription drugs to keep their mood fluctuations under control. They like to go with home remedies.

Home remedies for curing depression are related to taking a diet that is good at improving mood. There are foods that help improve serotonin level secretion in the brain naturally.

So, anyone who is depressed needs to eat healthy food. Anyone who is put on a healthy diet for a couple of weeks, will exhibit an overall improvement in mood and depression. Home remedies are not a one-time solution. They need to be practiced in a sustained manner. They can contribute to an overall cure and improvement when practiced for the long term. Most of the home remedies are about good food. So, a healthy dietary plan goes a long way in helping with depression and in dealing with the overall quality of health of the person.

When you have decent cognitive skills, you will definitely have a good mood. Foods that contain calcium, chromium, omega-3 fatty acids, vitamin B6, vitamin B12, vitamin D, folate, iron, magnesium, and zinc are mood boosters.

Try including foods like sweet potatoes, avocados, flax, broccoli, hemp, walnuts, greens and a range of other mood enhancing foods as a part of your regular diet to achieve sustained mood stability.

When you ensure regular intake of foods that are rich in these nutrients, you will be able to achieve a happy mood.

Mood is mostly dependent upon the different types of signals created by the brain. When someone is put on a healthy diet, their brain exhibits better powers of reasoning, which makes a great difference in their overall powers of reasoning, and of course the resultant decision making in overall life is improved. Good cognition leads to decreased depression and better mental health.

When the degree of depression is mild to moderate, psychotherapy and cognitive behavioral therapy would be of great help. However, when the degree of depression is too high the therapist might choose to go for electric shock treatment.

Psychotherapy

Psychotherapy helps one to get rid of troublesome thought patterns, inappropriate behavior, compulsive thoughts, and a wide range of emotions and conceptions that influence your relationship, work and social behavior for good.

Most of the problems that one does face in life are caused due to differences in opinion about life techniques one chooses to follow in life. Psychotherapy is mostly a session scheduled between the patient and the therapist. However, in cases where a coordinated effort would help with solving the issue the therapy sessions can be organized in groups or it can include the members of your family or work place.

The major goal of psychotherapy is to help people to change certain behavior patterns. The behavior that is being treated can be something that is required for the betterment of everyday life. There are different techniques and protocols that the therapist would choose to use to help with specific symptoms. It differs between therapists. These sessions are tailor made to suit the requirements of the specific patient. Psychotherapy helps with improving the coping mechanisms of the patient. An overall improvement in cognition with a positive outlook in life is as well established.

Cognitive-Behavioral Therapy

Cognitive behavioral therapy is mainly focused on changing the patterns of thinking in a person, and is used in cases of patients with obsessive thought patterns, which can eventually lead to undesirable or unhealthy social behavior.

Cognitive behavioral therapy becomes necessary when a person develops a regular flow of disturbing unwanted thoughts. These thought patterns can be hard to control. They can even be senseless. They can be unproductive and time consuming.

Patterns of thoughts relating to too much orderliness, precision, religious practices, doubt, aggression, contamination, idiotic themes, obsessed sexual thoughts and more can be unnecessarily overwhelming. Cognitive behavioral therapy is meant to identify unnecessary thought patterns that are reducing the overall quality of life of the patient. The therapist provides therapy to change the thought patterns of the patient to eventually achieve a positive cognitive pattern.

Eventually, the patient learns to look at life from a new perspective and to achieve balance and peace in their life.

Electric Shock Treatment

Electric shock treatment is a method where a brief seizure is created in the brain.

The main goal of this electric shock treatment is to bring in some changes in the brain chemistry, thereby reversing a specific mental illness. This method is used in extreme cases of mental illness where other treatments have failed to help.

Traditionally, electric shock treatment led to serious side effects, because the doses of electricity that were given were too high. These shock treatments were administered without anesthesia. This led to loss of memory. The bones were fractured. Serious side effects were seen. However, with advancement in technology, electric shock therapy is quite safe these days.

This treatment is found to be particularly helpful in cases of severe depression and higher end mental disorder where the patient has detached from reality leading to conditions like psychosis. This treatment is very commonly given, in cases, where the patient is expressing continual desire to commit suicide and is refusing to eat.

Extreme end psychiatric conditions that affect the overall quality of life are considered for this treatment method.

Chapter V: Simple Life Hacks

How meditation helps?

Mindful meditation goes a long way in helping one deal with depression. Meditation is indeed accepted as a modern medicine to help with depression.

Anyone who is depressed is going to come up with a happy story after practicing reliable meditation techniques for a reasonable amount of time.

Depression happens due to the lack of will power. Meditation is the quickest way to build your will power. If you thought meditation is only for monks, you are mistaken. Meditation is for anyone and everyone who is willing to build up their courage and confidence to proceed on a creative path.

Mindful meditation is a very common technique to help cure depression. All you have to do is to sit upright and concentrate on the present situation. You need to feel your breath. You need to allow thoughts to flow through you. Practice this meditation for 15 minutes a day.

Mindfulness is a very effective pain killer. Meditation can change your attitude from inside out. This can change the way you live and work.

Learn the technique

Thoughtful breathing while you are sitting upright with your eyes closed is one of the easiest meditation techniques you can follow to cure depression.

Practice this method for just 15 minutes a day. You are going to become more cool and collected. No matter how chaotic your environment might be, you will develop the ability to stay connected.

In this method, you need not pray to any God, visualize any kind of chakra or recite a mantra in a language that you are not familiar with. The simple idea is to concentrate on your breath.

You simply pay attention to your breath. When you do this, you should concentrate on the physical aspects of breathing. It is natural for your mind to wander and to shift the focus from breathing to your thoughts. When you realize your concentration has shifted from your breathing to your thoughts just come back again to concentrate on your breath.

When you focus on your thoughts you need to simply be non-judgmental about your thoughts and you have to get mindful about your breath over again. Repeat this over and over again. You will get used to this routine within 4 to 5 sessions.

The idea of dealing with depression by mindful meditation is to help you live in the now. Depressive events are either from the past or they are related to your panic of what might happen in the future. When you do not bother about the past or the future then you probably choose to live in the present. If you are living in the present, you are going to be doing what you should be doing exactly in the present moment.

"Live in the Current Minute"

Being mindful of where you are and living your life by the minute can help you to focus in a better way on your job.

You will gain a refreshed ability to understand what is going on in your head. The thoughts that divert you from being able to focus on your breathing can be casual, eventful, or even painful thoughts. The idea of mindfulness is about making you feel all these sensations without allowing them to control you.

You will improve your emotional intelligence and you will be able to deal with the situation with more clarity, without any kind of judgment. You will not deal with the issues from the point of fear or greed. You will be clear about your benefits. When you are mindful of what you are doing, you develop a very strong immune system. Your power of concentration will be greatly improved.

No matter how hard you try, the mind is set to wander. However, with repeated practice, you will be able to see that you are able to get back to concentrating on your breathing, rather than getting caught up in a new thought each time.

This is one of the elementary, yet powerful, meditation techniques you can practice while you are sitting, standing, or even when you are attending an official meeting. Concentrating on one inhalation and one exhalation as and when you can is a great start if you are too busy. Concentrate for just one minute in the beginning, and you can increase your minutes to hours with practice.

Distraction Method

When you encounter an event that will probably heat you up, a simple method is to distract yourself. You do not want to participate in the conversation, activity or event. You simply choose to walk away. You can choose to have a distracting activity like walking, running, jogging, playing music, listening to music, cleaning up a spot in your home or any other activity that keeps you from getting involved in the unpleasant situation.

Yoga / Exercise

Talk to your yoga instructor and learn a set of yoga techniques to practice when you are depressed. Practicing Sun Salutation is a great way to get your energy level going. Try to practice techniques that activate the spine. Simple stretch exercises can help. Reflexology massages in the acupressure points of your arms and legs go a long way. Having a refreshing head massage and a hot bath is also a way to divert from depressing thoughts. All these methods can help one get away from unwanted episodes. Even if you have encountered depressive episodes, these practices will help you get rid of the after effects.

Vent it out

Put down your thoughts on a piece of paper, without editing. Talk out your feelings with your friends. However, do not revive the same old regrets in your conversation over and over again. The idea is to get rid of depression.

Dietary & Lifestyle Changes

Quality of life is that which is generated from good food. Having a healthy eating plan is important to keep you charged with the energy you need for your life style. Food fuels your thought patterns as well. Therefore, ensure you have a nutritious lifestyle to suit the activity patterns of your life.

This area is comprehensively covered in the next chapter, with a bonus surprise!

Chapter VI: BONUS! Dietary changes to cure depression

Serotonin

Secretion of serotonin can be greatly helped by the wise intake of carbohydrate. You need to consume carbohydrate strategically. When you eat your carbohydrates, you should have them without any kind of guilt.

Serotonin is a neurotransmitter. It's also known as the happy molecule. This neurotransmitter is important in maintaining a happy mood. Most depressive episodes are related to decreased synthesis of serotonin.

Psychiatrists prescribe SSRIs. These drugs are a class of drugs known as Selective Serotonin Reuptake Inhibitors. These drugs increase the level of serotonin in the brain. Unfortunately, a drug-based increase in serotonin levels does not work all the time.

Increasing serotonin levels naturally, goes a long way to helping one deal with depression.

A simple idea would be to eat foods that are rich in serotonin. However, that is not the way it works. This is because serotonin in food sources like walnuts, hickory nuts, pineapple, tomato, plums, kiwis, and bananas does not cross the blood brain barrier. So serotonin levels do not simply increase by taking foods rich in serotonin.

Tryptophan is a precursor of serotonin. If you are going to take foods that are rich in Tryptophan, it is going to act as a precursor of serotonin. The selective intelligence of the body will create the required quantity of serotonin when the neurologic signals call for release of serotonin by using the precursors.

One idea is to supplement your diet with foods that have the amino acids that can serve as the raw material for serotonin synthesis. The complication here is that protein prevents the formation of serotonin. Therefore, more than what you eat - how you eat matters.

The key is when your body has the raw materials to synthesize Serotonin, when you are going to take pure carbohydrate food without any kind of emotional guilt in the eating process, this can lead to the neurological process that triggers serotonin synthesis.

If you are planning to help your body synthesize serotonin, the key is to supplement your diet with tryptophan and after sometime eat a bit of pure carbohydrate without guilt.

Dopamine

Dopamine synthesis is made possible by providing the body with the required amount of amino acid precursor to synthesize Dopamine. Decreasing the amount of sugars is important to improve the brain function. Increased sugars interfere with the brain chemistry.

Phenylalanine is one of the important amino acids that the body will need for the synthesis of dopamine. Improving on the neurotransmitter levels of the Central Nervous System, especially of dopamine and serotonin, is achieved by providing the brain with the required amounts of precursors.

While providing a diet rich in precursors and supplements is important, triggering the neurological reflexes to synthesize the neurotransmitters happens only from external triggers and life style activities.

You need to have a healthy routine for work and rest. When you have a healthy routine, the brain rewires a strategic plan to synthesize the essential neurotransmitters accordingly.

People with a healthy routine for work, recreation, and rest get going in a healthy manner without depressive episodes.

Eat Away the Daily Blues!

Carbohydrates are a very important trigger for the synthesis of mind boosting neurotransmitters like serotonin, which leads to daily blues. When you crave carbohydrates, try to eat some carbohydrate without feelings of guilt. A craving for carbohydrate is closely related to low-serotonin levels.

It is very important that you choose your carbohydrates wisely. Choose to have food stuff that is made up of complex carbohydrates, which are whole grains.

- Ready to eat snacks, made of whole grains like snack crackers and popcorn are healthy snacking options to keep away your blues.
- Fresh juices of beetroot, mixed berries, orange, green apple, carrots, lemon, cucumber, spinach, celery, cabbage, ginger, red apple or any fruit or veggie juice for that reason can kick your blues away.

You can choose to have recipes made up of brown rice, buckwheat, bulgur, millet, oatmeal, popcorn, quinoa, and rolled oats. Whole grain foods are made up of grains with barn, endosperm, and germ. If one of these elements is missing then you cannot call it a whole grain.

Multi-grain, stone-ground, 100% wheat, cracked wheat, seven grain, and barn are not whole grain, because they lose one or more of the barn, endosperm or germ.

Any meal that is prepared with whole grains, helps to keep away daily blues. When you make them a part of your daily diet routine, you will see that you are able to consistently keep away from the blues.

Conclusion

The surest way to treat yourself is to first have the right knowledge about the issue, and we hope this Book has served the purpose. Feel free to use the information in any order to cure your depression, or help a loved one fight depression with the tips and tricks that you've just learnt.

Remember, when depression creeps in, ask for help. Help is available everywhere.

I sincerely wish you and your loved ones good mental health.

Good luck!

www.ingramcontent.com/pod-product-compliance
Lightning Source LLC
Chambersburg PA
CBHW072027280526
45788CB00007B/2706